Greater Than a Tourist Boo

I think the series is wonderful and beneficial for tourists to get information before visiting the city.

-Seckin Zumbul, Izmir Turkey

I am a world traveler who has read many trip guides but this one really made a difference for me. I would call it a heartfelt creation of a local guide expert instead of just a guide.

-Susy, Isla Holbox, Mexico

New to the area like me, this is a must have!

-Joe, Bloomington, USA

This is a good series that gets down to it when looking for things to do at your destination without having to read a novel for just a few ideas.

-Rachel, Monterey, USA

Good information to have to plan my trip to this destination.

-Pennie Farrell, Mexico

Aptly titled, you won't just be a tourist after reading this book. You'll be greater than a tourist!

-Alan Warner, Grand Rapids, USA

Thank you for a fantastic book.

-Don, Philadelphia, USA

Sohaila Ammar

Great ideas for a port day.
-Mary Martin USA

Even though I only have three days to spend in San Miguel in an upcoming visit, I will use the author's suggestions to guide some of my time there. An easy read - with chapters named to guide me in directions I want to go.
-Robert Catapano, USA

Great insights from a local perspective! Useful information and a very good value!
-Sarah, USA

This series provides an in-depth experience through the eyes of a local. Reading these series will help you to travel the city in with confidence and it'll make your journey a unique one.
-Andrew Teoh, Ipoh, Malaysia

Tourists can get an amazing "insider scoop" about a lot of places from all over the world. While reading, you can feel how much love the writer put in it.
-Vanja Živković, Sremski Karlovci, Serbia

GREATER THAN A TOURIST – ALEXANDRIA EGYPT

50 Travel Tips from a Local

Sohaila Ammar

Sohaila Ammar

Cover Image: https://pixabay.com/en/egypt-alexandria-bey-citadel-1289497/

Greater Than a Tourist
Visit our website at www.GreaterThanaTourist.com

Lock Haven, PA
All rights reserved.
ISBN: 9781980419563

>TOURIST

50 TRAVEL TIPS FROM A LOCAL

Sohaila Ammar

BOOK DESCRIPTION

Are you excited about planning your next trip?
Do you want to try something new?
Would you like some guidance from a local?

If you answered yes to any of these questions, then this Greater Than a Tourist book is for you.

Greater Than a Tourist- Alexandria Egypt by Sohaila Ammar offers the inside scoop on Alexandria. Most travel books tell you how to travel like a tourist. Although there is nothing wrong with that, as part of the Greater Than a Tourist series, this book will give you travel tips from someone who has lived at your next travel destination.

In these pages, you will discover advice that will help you throughout your stay. This book will not tell you exact addresses or store hours but instead will give you excitement and knowledge from a local that you may not find in other smaller print travel books.

Travel like a local. Slow down, stay in one place, and get to know the people and the culture. By the time you finish this book, you will be eager and prepared to travel to your next destination.

Sohaila Ammar

TABLE OF CONTENTS

DEDICATION

This book is dedicated to Ahmed, my friend, husband, and partner who made my life brighter just by being in it. No thanks will ever be enough for all what he did to support me in every step including my decision to switch my career and become a writer. I also want to thank my friends who became family to me: Eman, Asmaa, and Abd El Mohsen, and my family who became my dearest friends: Doha, Salma, Sara, my amazing nephew Omar, niece Sama, and last but not least my caring two aunts Magda & Hanan. Every one of them has been more than supportive and a rock for me to lean on when I needed and no words will ever be able to describe my love and gratitude towards them.

Sohaila Ammar

ABOUT THE AUTHOR

Sohaila is an Egyptian writer who lives in Alexandria. She was born and lived most of her life in the city. After years of traveling and trying new cities, she had to return to her beloved Alexandria as she realized how difficult it is to live without seeing the Mediterranean every morning, walk its shores or the streets of the ancient city. She loves to read, explore, and write her own vision of the world.

Sohailaloves to travel for knowledge and experience as well as fun. In her travels she makes sure to spend the time to get to know the people as well as the place, to learn their culture and try to understand the reasons behind their achievements, dreams, and beliefs.

Sohaila Ammar

HOW TO USE THIS BOOK

The Greater Than a Tourist book series was written by someone who has lived in an area for over three months. The goal of this book is to help travelers either dream or experience different locations by providing opinions from a local. The author has made suggestions based on their own experiences. Please do your own research before traveling to the area in case the suggested places are unavailable.

Sohaila Ammar

FROM THE PUBLISHER

Traveling can be one of the most important parts of a person's life. The anticipation and memories that you have are some of the best. As a publisher of the Greater Than a Tourist book series, as well as the popular 50 Things to Know book series, we strive to help you learn about new places, spark your imagination, and inspire you. Wherever you are and whatever you do I wish you safe, fun, and inspiring travel.

Lisa Rusczyk Ed. D.
CZYK Publishing

Sohaila Ammar

OUR STORY

Traveling is a passion of the "Greater than a Tourist" series creator. Lisa studied abroad in college, and for their honeymoon Lisa and her husband toured Europe. During her travels to Malta, an older man tried to give her some advice based on his own experience living on the island since he was a young boy. She was not sure if she should talk to the stranger but was interested in his advice. When traveling to some places she was wary to talk to locals because she was afraid that they weren't being genuine. Through her travels, Lisa learned how much locals had to share with tourists. Lisa created the "Greater Than a Tourist" book series to help connect people with locals. A topic that locals are very passionate about sharing.

Sohaila Ammar

WELCOME TO
> TOURIST

Sohaila Ammar

INTRODUCTION

Travel is the one thing of all experiences you could think of that will open your eyes and mind to the world, make you a better person, and enable you to see all the great possibilities of life, the world, and even yourself and other people. Once you decide to start traveling and get a taste of that life-changing experience, you will find no similar pleasure to that of getting to visit new places, unveil the mysteries of foreign cultures and ancient civilizations like those of Alexandria, the city in which I've lived for a big portion of my life. So, get started and let the travel bug give you its bite of adventure. Who knows? Maybe it will be the reason for you to find yourself and your place in this wide world.

Sohaila Ammar

1. FEEL FREE TO HAVE THAT FAMOUS TOURIST LOOK

Unlike other cities, Alexandria welcomes foreign visitors who are interested in its seashore sites, Hellenistic monuments, and Islamic architecture. The people of Alexandria are accustomed to the sight of tourists, whether they are in groups or individuals, walking around in their shorts with their cameras and fanny packs. The locals in Alexandria do not avoid socializing with tourists, on the contrary, are always prepared and happy to answer your questions for directions to the place you're headed or recommendations for nearby restaurants.

Egypt in general as a country is famous for its hospitality, historical sites, and leisure spots,as tourism represents a major part of the country's national income,it is quite common for the locals to see tourists walking around in a tourism site or in a local area.

This is not an invitation to roam the local areas alone late at night of course. Feel free to stay out as late as you like as long as you are in a busy tourist site or a club, but local areas, like any other place in the world, is where the people of the city live their lives so they won't be very happy to have strangers or noise at a late hour.

2. DIVIDE AND CONQUER

Being a tourist in a city like Alexandria rich with activities to do and sites to visit, you can easily lose precious time of your trip moving from one site to the next if you did not divide your visits in a smart way. This is why you have to decide in advance on how you want to spend your time and where; you also have to make these decisions for each day separately. Make accurate plans for the places you want to visit and make sure to search the geographic location of every one of them so that you are able to gather all sites in one area, or areas that are close to each other, in the same day in order to spend most of your day in one region. This way you will not waste more time than you necessarily need on transportations and traffic.

Of course, the traffic in Alexandria is not monstrous as it is in Cairo, the Capitol of the country, but still, you are in the second largest city in Egypt and you most probably will be limited by the few days of your stay in the city and that's why the time and location planning is important to get the most out of your visit time.

3. HAVE A FRIEND IN THE CITY

This is probably the most important tip of them all since the people of Alexandria speak Arabic, the formal language of the country and since Arabic is somewhat strange to the foreign ear, especially the western ear, and it is not easy to pick up on it. Attempting to learn a new language, especially a language that has strange sounds, to say the least like Arabic, for a trip is not a reasonable thing to consider. With the need to have a clear understanding of what is going on around you, the easiest available way to achieve that is to have someone who understands and preferably speak the common tongue.

Having an Alexandrian, or at least Egyptian, friend will be of a great help when it comes to dividing your visits based on areas like I mentioned in the previous tip, he or she will have the knowledge of the best places to buy souvenirs at better prices as well as the ability to dealing with the local sellers which will allow you to buy things at the local prices rather than the "tourist price".

If you don't already have a friend in the city, go ahead and make one, it is really easy and you will find that the Alexandrian people will welcome the idea and offer much help. Use Facebook to meet new people from Alexandria before you arrive, this way you will have a friend to guide you and help you to experience the city form a local point of view.

4. USE AIRBNB FOR ACCOMMODATIONS

Hotels are nice, there is no question in that, especially during a vacation when you just want to relax and have almost everything available at one place, staying in a hotel is the obvious choice with all the different services they offer and entertainment facilities within, and Alexandria has some of the best hotels in all of Egypt, so if what you are looking for is just a traditional accommodation for your trip and budget is not an issue for you, you can stay in the famous Four Seasons, the Plaza, Azur, or any other big 5-star options which will all have a sea view and professional crews at your service. But if you do have a budget which you do not intend to spend on just a place to sleep at night, then my advice to you is to go on Airbnb, find yourself a pleasant inn or better yet a room in one of the locals' homes.You will find this to be a great opportunity to experience the city from an angle

17

that you'll never get while staying in a 5-star hotel room. Living in a local residential area, even if it was for a little while, and walking the streets of where the people actually live their lives will give you the experience which is the true essence of travel, it will allow you achieve that goal of opening your mind to new habits, new ways of thinking, and a new way of living. Have no worries, hotels will still be there for when you desire to spend a luxurious night partying or try a special restaurant in one of those fancy hotels.

5. TRY A LOCAL COFFEE SHOP (QAHWA BALADY)

In the past, local coffee shops were strictly a place for men with a few exceptions that would receive female guests especially if they were tourists out of the city and the country in general. Things are much easier nowadays though, Local coffee shops open their doors for both genders in every possible area in Alexandria which creates a wonderful opportunity for tourists to mix and mingle with the locals in one of the most authentic pleasure places for the locals of the city. I have to advise you to not get your hopes up about the luxury of those local coffee shops though; you will most likely find the place to be simply furnished with wooden or plastic chairs and tables that are made of a mix of steel and old marble. You will have to make your peace with the noise too as it is one of the noisiest places you could visit in the city because of the sounds of the crowd talking, laughing, and playing backgammon or domino, the two most popular games in every local coffee shop in Alexandria. Take the chance to ask one of the locals there to teach you how to play them, you'll find it to be quite fun.

A local coffee shop, pronounced "qahwa" in Arabic which is the same name for "coffee" in the language as well, is the perfect place for you to try your first "Shisha" or hookah.

6. SPEND A DAY BY THE MEDITERRANEAN

Alexandria is most famous among all other Egyptian cities for being a coastal city. Although this is the case of many other cities in Egypt like Hurghada, Prot Said, Sharm El Sheikh, and Dahab, all those cities are on the coast of the Red Sea and while other cities in Egypt lay on the coast of the Mediterranean and are quite good for a summertime visit like Marsa Matrouh, only in the case of Alexandria you can enjoy being in a coastal city that is considered to be central as well since it is the second largest city and the second Capitol of the historically rich country. So, while spending your vacation in Alexandria do not miss the chance to enjoy a long sitting by the sea in one of the cafes that are built directly on top of the rocks along the beach, or on the sand beaches of the eastern side of the city. Order a soft drink or a tea with mint alongside your favorite flavor of "Shisha" if you enjoy smoking, and you will find yourself easily relaxed at the sight of the blue charming waters so much so that you may find yourself not wanting to leave, and in that situation I would suggest you order your next meal from a nearby restaurants and spend the rest of your day with the company of the Mediterranean.

7. EAT FISH BY THE SEA IN "EL MAX"

When it comes to having an authentic local experience in Alexandria, this is one of the most important tips of all. This one is about FOOD! Local food right out of the Mediterranean Sea and cooked by a local woman. This particular experience will give you the closest taste of an Alexandrian home cooking you can get in a restaurant.

In the area of "El Max" in the West of Alexandria lays "El Llol" restaurant for fish and seafood. The restaurant is right in the middle of the cabins of the fishermen of El Max and right on the sand beach. The place is built in the shape of a ship and it is built of wood that came out of actual boats; do not let that intimidate you though, it is very strong and very secure place that stood for tens of years.

Inside that ship you will be able to choose your own fish one by one as well as choosing how you'd like them to be cooked. Then, you decide whether you will sit inside of the ship or outside on the sand beach to have your meal in front of the beacon of El Max. The food, as I mentioned before is cooked by a local woman who is, in fact, the wife of the owner "El Llol" himself.

8. TAKE A WALK IN "FOUAD STREET"

Fouad Street is one of the oldest and most important streets of Alexandria. The street was first founded during the Ptolemaic period before Christ and was named the "Canopic Road" because columns of marble stood on both of its sides from the top of the road and all the way down it. The name of the street was changed later in the beginning of the 20th century to have the same name as the king of Egypt at the time, Fouad I who died in 1936. Located in the center of the historical city, Fouad Street carries its own history as it represents the fusion of cultures that Alexandria witnessed between Greek, Armenians, and Italians. Filled with high ancient buildings that were built according to the ancient Greek style mixed with a touch of the architectural art of Florence, Italy, the architecture of the street alone is worth a trip to it on foot to enjoy the sight of the old buildings and its decorations that will give you the feeling of taking a trip in time itself.

If you decide to put the history of the place aside, which would be a little hard to do in the city of Alexandria in general, Fouad Street nowadays is filled with entertainment facilities like museums, movie theaters, old diverse flower shops that give the street a beauty of a classy kind, and many restaurants that have a large rang of cuisines to satisfy every taste and craving. So, no matter what you might need, you can and will find in Fouad Street.

9. VISIT THE MUSEUM OF THE SUNKEN MONUMENTS

Alexandria owns what may be the first museum for sunken monuments in the world thanks to an Alexandrian archaeologist and diver who discovered a large number of monuments, over 2000 pieces, at the bottom of the sea in the Eastern Port which is located in the area of Abu Quir. The sunken pieces under the water of the Mediterranean were discovered in the year 1933 and were identified as the remains of old cities that once stood in the place. The collection of the sunken museum contains a variety of coins, jewelry, and whole statues that kept its condition despite the years it spent under the sea, as well as pieces of old statues remains. Most of the sunken treasures go back to the times of the Pharos and the Ptolemaic period. In addition to the small pieces which you can see in the Graeco-Roman museum to which it was transferred, there still is a number of remains of sunken ships, remains of ancient palaces, and fortresses as well as the last pieces that remain from the Lighthouse of Alexanderia which was located in the western side of the city and was once one of the seven ancient wonders of the world. For those amazing treasures you would have to dive into the sea in a one of a kind adventure to behold those enchanting remains where the people of Alexandria and the cities before once lived while others only hoped to visit.

10. VISIT THE CITADEL OF QAITBAY

Also known as Fort Qaitbay, the Citadel that stands on the far western end of the coast of the Mediterranean was built by Sultan Qaitbay in the 14th century to defend the shores of Alexandria against the attacks of the Ottoman Empire. Some of the Granit stones that was used in building the Citadel of Qaitbay was taken from the ruins of the legendry Lighthouse of Alexandria that was built in the same location centuries before by the Pharos and was destroyed over the years by sequential earthquakes that hit its location over the years.

The strategic location of the fortress allowed it to act once more as a defend line for the city hundreds of years later during the British attack on Alexandria in 1882, as Egyptian officers and patriots took shelter in it during the bombarding of the Alexandrian shore by the British ships, although it was in vain, the Citadel of Qaitbay still stands to this day as a witness to the bravery of the people of this great city. The Citadel is, of course, no longer used for its original military purpose; it opens its doors daily for visitors who enjoy examining its architecture and some of the old weapons that remains in it, and for those who like to enjoy the sea and just want to sit in the shadow of its walls.

11. VISIT THE ROYAL JEWLERY MUSEUM

In the elegant area named Zizinia in the city of Alexandria you will find the museum that displays the jewelry of the last royal family to every rule Egypt, "Muhammad Ali" Family .Also called the palace of Jewelry, the museum is in fact the palace of the former princess and a descendant of "Muhammad Ali", "Fatima Al Zahra'" and it was transformed into a museum in 1986 after almost 30 years of the cope that ended the royal rule of Egypt in 1952. The palace was originally founded by Fatima Al Zahra's mother, Zienab Fahmy back in 1919 following the European style of architecture. The palace, now museum, consists of two wings, Eastern and western, connected by a hallway. Each of the wings contains two levels as well as a basement. The building is surrounded by a beautiful garden filled with trees and different kinds of flowers. All of this makes the architecture and atmosphere of the museum is an enough of a reason to pay the place a visit, so when you add the fact that the museum contains over 11,000 pieces of the jewelry that once belonged to the royal family of Egypt which makes it rare in design and majestic to behold, then you know for sure that you would be missing a lot to be in Alexandria and not to go to the museum of royal jewelry.

12. TAKE A STROLL IN "EL MONTAZAH"

Since we started talking about the remaining properties of the last royal family of Egypt that got opened for visitors, we have to mention El Montazah. El Montazah, which translates from Arabic to "the park". El Montazah was originally the official summer palace for the royal family members to spend the hot summer days in on the shore of the Mediterranean. Founded by King Abbas Helmy in 1892, El Montazah started with only one palace that was called "El Salamlek" which means:"the place for quiet and peace" as well as a very large garden which King Abbas Helmy supervised its design in person. Later during the rule of kings Fouad I and his son King Farouk I, more palaces were built for the queen and the princesses called "El Haramlek" which means "the place for women", A bridge was also built to connect the gardens with the "Island of Tea" in the Mediterranean, in addition to another extension of the gardens, a royal train station, a cinema for the princesses, and offices for the employees who managed the estate.

Nowadays the gardens of El Montazah and all the palaces it contains are open for visitors. I'll have to warn you, though, the gardens are quite extensive and to explore all of it you will have to do a great deal of walking, which I recommend since the place is beautiful and you will be able to enjoy it more on foot, or you can just get a car if you would like to save yourself the effort.

El Montazah also has four gorgeous beaches: Aida, Cleopatra, Venice, and Semiramis, as well as a private beach of Palestine Hotel which, by the way, would be a great opportunity to enjoy the gardens of El Montazah, the beach, and the stay in the hotel combined.

13. A PICTURE IS WORHT A THOUSAND WORDS

This is a common advice that applies on any trip you may take. As a tourist, you most probably will see the place and its people only for this one time during your visit. Pictures are the one true reminder that lasts from any good time you spend, and when this time is spent in a rich city like Alexandria, you have to take many colorful pictures at every site you get to visit starting with pictures of the gorgeous Mediterranean Sea, and every single historical site in the city, even a picture or two of yourself smoking hookah will be a whimsical memory of your trip.

14. EAT ICE CREAM AT EL NEZAMY'S

El Nezamy is an old Alexandrian Ice Cream shop that is located in the famous area of Bahary on the western end of "El Courniesh". The shop is a small one and it offers specific desert items on its menu and every single item tastes absolute heaven. Besides the various ice cream flavors that the shop prepares in a way that guarantee carries an original fresh taste of the fruit the ice cream is flavored with, you can try "Roz belaban" which is an Egyptian kind of dessert that is made with sweetened rice cooked in milk, yet my personal recommendation for you is to try the mix of the rice milk and ice cream with a topping of crunchy nuts.

15. HAVE A FOUL & FALAFEL BREAKFAST

Foul, if you are not familiar with it, is basically beans that get slowly cooked and then seasoned with different spices, lemon, and hot oil, while Falafel, which is much more famous, is the same kind of beans that Foul is made of but peeled and crushed into a soft paste then seasoned with garlic, coriander, and other ingredients, then the mixture is fried in oil to form those delicious crunchy famous circles with sesame seeds on top.

There are tons of places where you can find Foul and Falafel since they form a very popular meal for the people of Alexandria for both breakfast and dinner. Some of the places where you can get the ultimate meal of Foul and Falafel are not that famous even to the local people of Alexandria and it depends on the area of the joint where it usually gets known only by its residents. "El Prince" for example is a little known place located in the area of Sidi Bishr, Mohamed Nageeb Street exactly, that serves the best Falafel I have ever tasted, so I strongly recommend it. This specific place is easy to get to since it is located on a main and a famous street in the city, so I recommend you get up early one day of your vacation in Alexandria, tell your driver the name of the street, and once you are there start your day with a crunchy, strong flavored, hot falafel.

16. DRINK COFFEE AT "THE BRAZILIAN COFFEE"

Turkish coffee is very popular in Alexandria and Egypt in general and to guarantee that you get the best cup of this coffee, you have to get it at the one of Brazilian coffee Stores.

The first Brazilian coffee store in Alexandria was founded in 1920 by a Greek man who lived in Alexandria like so many others at the time, so the store is not really Brazilian since the owner who equipped it with a The cappuccino machine that is said to be the first one in the world; it is just a name for the brand. Nevertheless, the man did know what he was doing because to this day the smell and taste of the freshly grounded coffee beans will make you feel like you are standing among the coffee trees.

The store has opened many branches all over Alexandria over the year, but the original store is located in Salah Salem Street.

17. ATTEND A CONCERT IN THE OPRA HOUSE

The opera In Alexandria, also known as "Saied Darweesh Theater", was founded during the 20s of the last century. The design of the theater was built to match the style of Vienna Opera and Odeon Theater in Paris. It was originally named after Muhammad Ali but the name was changed to "Saied Darweesh" who is a very famous pioneer Alexandrian musician.

After many years of not working the historic Theater came back to life in 2004 and elegant concerts and Ballets started to be held in it once more after restoring its beauty and glory. So, try to catch a performance in the elegant theater, even if there will be singing and you can't understand the language, I promise that you will enjoy the elegance and beauty of the music.

18. VISIT THE LIBRARY OF ALEXANDRIA

The Library of Alexandria (Bibliotheca Alexandrina) was built in 2002 as a recreation of the ancient library of Alexandria which was built during the rule of Ptolemy I and was called "the royal library" and was the largest one in the world of its time. The new Library was built with the help of the UN in a location near the one where the ancient library once stood.

The Library of Alexandria consists of many levels and contains seven specialized sections as well as several museums; each museum contains a very rich content according to its specialty.

In a separate sphere-shaped building is the Planetarium that contains the history of sciences museum inside the inverted pyramid as a tribute to all scientists whose work over the centuries have contributed to the human knowledge.

Bibliotheca Alexandrina holds many events every month including children activities and displaying of films.

19. VISIT ABU AL-ABBAS AL-MURSI MOSQUE

The locals call it "El Morsi Mosque", the mosque contains the tomb of Andalusi Sufi saint "Shehab Adeen Abu Al-Abbas Al-Morsi" who lived and died in Alexandria for 43 years in the 13th century. The decorations of the mosque is on both Arabic and Andalusi styles with pillars of marble and copper and under its western dome of the mosque is the tombs of Abu Al-Abbas and his two sons.

On top of the mosque is the minaret, a slender tower with a balcony that is used to announce prayer times and call Muslim people for prayer. The man who calls for prayers, Al muezzin, used to climb the stairs and stand in the balcony to say the call to prayer as loud as possible for the people to hear, but now microphone are used for that purpose and al muezzin call to the five prayers of the day from inside the mosque.

During the call for prayer Muslims are supposed to stay quiet, listen to the phrases of the call, and repeat them in a low voice. As a non Muslim tourist you are under no obligation to do so of course, but I recommend that you listen and enjoy the beautiful voice of Al muezzin as he calls.

20. TRY KUSHARI ABU NASER

During the 19th century Egypt was a hub for many cultures of the people who lived in it including Indians and Italians. When the economic crisis of that century hit Kushari was developed in Egypt as a cheap filling dish from the Indian dish "Khichdi" which is rice and lentils with the addition of the Italian macaroni and an Egyptian red sauce. The dish gained several additions over the years like crunchy fried onions and chickpeas and an additional condiment made from garlic and vinegar.

Koshari is now a very popular dish all over Egypt, and for the best Kushari in Alexandria, I recommend a local restaurant that specializes in local foods called Abu Nasser. The place started out strictly serving kushari and then added all of its other menu items as it expanded. Abu Nasser is very famous in Al-Mansheia area and very easy to go to.

21. WALK AROUND THE RAML STATION AND MANSHEIA

Side by side, those two neighborhoods are the heart of the city and the original center it started from. Raml Station square is the first square in Alexandria and the station itself was the first station from when the tram first came and started working in Alexandria. The station was designed by the Italian Architect Antonio Lasciac in 1887 and was visited by many celebrities over the years including Elvis Presley, Agatha Christy, Demis Roussos, the boxing champion Muhammad Ali, and many others who were taken by the beauty of the Raml Station square and Alexandria. The neighborhood's two main streets, Saad Zaghlool and Saphia Zaghloul, are filled with book stores, gift shops, and restaurants. Also Saphia Zaghloul Street is a direct link to Fouad Street and if you keep walking you will get to another historical location which is the Roman Amphitheatre of Alexandria.

Mansheia neighborhood on the other hand is less of a tourist attraction since it does not have much other than The Unknown Naval Soldier Memorial to visit, yet it is a great opportunity to mix with the locals and get to know them because it has one of the most famous markets of Alexandria in Faransa "France" Street, and "Zan2et El Setat".

22. VISIT THE MUSEUM OF FINE ARTS

The Museum of Fine Arts was founded when a German Citizen, Edward Fred Heim, gave the city of Alexandria 210 paintings and other pieces that were created by international artist as a gift on a condition that the city would allocate a special place to display them otherwise they would be sent back to Germany to be displayed in a museum in Dusseldorf. Responding to Fred Heim's condition, a villa in Moharam Bek neighborhood was donated to the city by an Alexandrian benefactor, Baron De Menasha, to be the museum where these pieces are displayed.

Now the museum exhibits three collections of fine art by Egyptian and international artists. The first collection is the 210 pieces that started the museum; the second collection which is exhibited separately on the second floor was donated by the Egyptian artist Mohamed Mahmoud Khalil, lastly the third collection was donated to the museum by the museum of modern art in Cairo.

23. SEE POMPEY'S PILLAR

Although the name might mislead you to think that this Pillar has something to do with Pompey, the Roman Consul who fled to Alexandria and was murdered by the Ptolemaic ruler then, the Pillar is not related to him. This mistake was made by the European crusaders who thought when they came to Alexandria that Pompey's head was put in a jar in the crown placed on the top of the Pillar. In fact the

Pillar, which is a 100 feet of red Granit that came all the way from Aswan in south standing on top of the rocky hill, was erect in 300 AD as a triumphal monument for the Roman Emperor Diocletain after Christianity triumphed in Alexandria.

24. VISIT THE ROMAN AMPHITHEATRE

Located in Kom El-Dekka neighborhood, The Roman Amphitheater is one of the most famous Roman monuments in Alexandria. The word Amphitheater means "double theater" and it is used to indicate the grand and impressive structure of the theater which is built in a half circle shape to be an open air theater with no curtains on its stage. The theater also contains several galleries that contained rooms as an additional place for more spectators other than the 800 seated in the marble seats that surrounded the stage.

The Roman Amphitheater is located at the end of Saphia Zaghloul Street and is opened for visitors except for official holidays.

25. VISIT THE GRAECO-ROMAN MUSEUM

The Graeco-Roman Museum was founded back in 1829 to hold a priceless collection of over 40,000 pieces including mosaics, coins, woodwork, sculptures, and other objects that are left form the Graeco-

Roman, also known as Ptolemaic, culture during the period when it mixed with the Egyptian culture after Alexander the Great conquest of Egypt in the third century BC.

The museum was first located in a five-room apartment in a small building on Horreya Road, but then was transferred to a larger building three years after it was founded in 1895.

The museum is opened daily from 9 AM to 4 PM except for Fridays when it is closed from 11:30 AM to 1:30 PM which is the duration of the Muslim prayer of Friday.

26. VISIT ALEXANDRIA NATIONAL MUSEUM

This particular museum is of great importance and its importance has been growing recently since it is the main official facility that documents the rich heritage of Alexandria, the Ptolemaic capital of Egypt. The museum was founded in 2003 to be the home for over 1800 artifacts that combined tells the story of Alexandria over the centuries of different cultures from the Pharaonic era, passing by the Roman, Coptic eras and finally reaching the Islamic era as well as a number of modern 19th century pieces from the time when Muhammad Ali and his descendents ruled Egypt including chinaware, glassware, and silverware that indicates the richness of this period. In addition to that there is a special underground room where several mummies are preserved and displayed and a dedicated floor for the pieces that were retrieved from under the sea.

27. DO NOT MISS ST. MARK CATHEDRAL

St. Mark the Evangelist was the author of the second Gospel. He was connected to the city of Alexandria from the early Christian era. Coptic Christians believe that St. Mark came to Alexandria in 60 AD and lived in the city for 6 years. During the years of his stay in Alexandria, St. Mark preformed many miracles and helped many souls to find their way to Christianity. He was the founder of the church of Alexandria and the first Bishop of the city. After his martyrdom, St. Mark was buried under the church he had founded.

The Cathedral that stands today in Raml Station Neighborhood is on the same site where the church St. Mark founded and it is the largest Cathedral in Alexandria.

28. VISIT MONASTERY OF ANBA PISHOY

The Monastery of Anba (Saint) Pishoy contains 5 churches; the main and largest church is named after Anba Pishoy and the other four are named after: Abaskhiron the Soldier, Mary, Saint George, and Archangel Michael. The monastery was built by Saint Pishoy himself in the 4th century. After his death, Pope Joseph I of Alexandria fulfilled the wish of Saint Pishoy to have his body and the body of Paul of Tammah to the monastery. Today the bodies of both Saints rest in the main church of the monastery. Eyewitnesses including Pope

Shenouda III of Alexandria said that the body of Saint Pishoy remains intact to this day.

A well known as the well of martyrs is in the monastery. According to Coptic history, this well was the burial place for 49 martyrs who were killed by the Berbers until Christians retrieved the bodies and gave them proper burials in the Monastery of Sain Macarius the Great.

29. DRINK SWEETCANE JUICE

If you are not familiar with sweetcane, it is bamboo-like sticks that grow in warm climates like India and Egypt.

Sweetcane is also known as sugarcane, the juice is the extract that comes out from sugarcanes when they are pressed. The word juice is a bit misleading, though, since sugarcane is not a fruit or a vegetable.

The sweet green-ish drink is very popular especially in hot weather. Only make sure to get it in a plastic cup with a straw.

30. GO ON A YACHT TRIP

Weekly yacht trips are arranged for the local people of Alexandria and tourists alike to enjoy the Mediterranean for an entire day while the yacht is taking its passengers from the eastern end of the coast of the city in Abu Qir and all the way to the western end of the coast in Bahary. These trip would be an amazing chance for a tourist to have an overview of the city from seaside as well as interacting with the locals on their leisure time during the trip. Yachts that go on those trips usually offers meals and drinks all day included in the price of the trip so, you won't have to worry about the details. Just bring your fun adventurous self and get going.

31. RIDE THE BIG RED BUS

This bus is rather new to Alexandria and the local people of the city are enjoying it as much as tourists are. Being the only bus in Alexandria that has two levels with the second level exposed to the fresh air and the sunny beautiful sky and with a bright red color the bus has been an attraction since it was brought to Alexandria a few years ago and a fun way to get around the city. The bus goes back and forth on the sea road between the two official stations at the two ends of the city: Mansheya, and Mandara. Unlike other buses, the big red bus does not really have stations to stop in, it stops for people to get on as the give the driver a sign that they like to get on the bus, and stops also for passengers to get off when they press the one of buttons on the bus to signal their wish to get off to the driver.

32. EAT SHAWERMA AT EL SULTAN AYOUB

If you are familiar with Middle Eastern food, then you know that gigantic skewer that gets stacked with layers of seasoned meat or chicken and rotates vertically in front of a fire until the meat or chicken is cooked and then sliced by a special chef whose only job is to make Shawerma. Shawerma is originally a Turkish dish that came to Egypt with the Ottoman conquest of the country and became a very popular food among Egyptians ever since.

There are Hundreds of Shawerma joints in Alexandria and every one of them differs in the marinate of the meat or chicken which changes the taste entirely from one spot to the other, but they all use the same traditional way of grilling in the vertical skewer.

Sultan Ayoub is one of the absolute best Shawerma joints in Alexandria. The people there have mastered the ultimate recipe for marinating the meat and they manage to get it right every single time. So, if you eat meat and decide to try Shawerma, I would definitely recommend Sultan Ayoub for that experience.

33. BUY GIFTS FROM "ZAN'ET EL SETAT"

"Zan'et El Setat" is one of the most famous markets in Alexandria in Mansheya neighborhood. Its name can be translated to "the crowded place of women". The markets name came from its narrow streets that is always crowded with women shoppers mostly as well as the fact that most of the goods in the market is of a feminine nature. Although most of the market's visitors are women, almost all the salesmen who work there are men but that seems not to bother the shoppers at all.

The history and foundation of the market goes back to the beginnings of the 19th century when traders from Morocco and Libya used to stay in Mansheya neighborhood when they came to Alexandria and do most of their trading in this market.

34. GO TO GREEN PLAZA AND SAN STEFANO

Since this book is about tips from a local to help you as a tourist enjoy your stay in the city in a unique manner that will help you explore the city and experience it from the point of view of one of its residents, it is important to pass through some of the regular places where people of the city go to for outings to have fun. One of the most popular places is Green Plaza. Green Plaza is a complex of stores, cinemas, an a wide variety of restaurants all spread over a vast land with wide open spaces where you can sit in open air cafes or rid the funny little train that roams the grounds and Alexandrians call "Taftaf".

San Stefano on the other hand is a regular mall but one of Alexandria's finest malls since it is attached to the Four Seasons hotel and residential apartments. Outside of the mall you will find many open air cafes by the seaside like Starbucks and Fresca.

35. SPEND A DAY AT THE NORTH COAST

The North coast of Egypt extends for more that 1000 kilometers along the shore of the Mediterranean Sea and in the center of it is the city of

Alexandria. The rest of the North Coast has been utilized in several resorts that were built and developed over the past decade or so until it got to a point today where those resorts have everything so that you do not have to cut out your leisure time to get something that is not available in the resort you are staying in. These resorts of the North Coast today are a great place for nightlife and partying during the summer.

36. EAT BEDOUIN FOOD AT "KHATAB OASIS"

Do not let the name mislead you; this is a restaurant for Bedouin food not a real oasis. Although you might feel like you have found an oasis after being lost in the middle of the desert when you try the food of this restaurant. First of all, let me note clearly that Khatab Oasis is no place for a vegetarian since its menu is mostly about meats. The restaurant which is located near Bourg El Arab neighborhood serves some of the best meats cooked in Bedouin style you will ever taste. From lamb rips and grilled kebab and "kufta" to stuffed pigeons and grilled chickens this place is capable of cooking any meat that comes to mind and make it taste heavenly with charcoal flavor even if what you ordered is an entire lamb... yes, they do grill fully intact lambs, so if you are in Alexandria and eat meat do not leave without having this experience.

37. EAT LOCAL EASTERN PIZZA

There is almost no chance that there is someone in the world who does not know pizza. But the pizza I'm talking about here is not the original Italian pizza or even the famous American one, although Alexandria has pizzerias that serve those two, you can still find them anywhere else in the world. The pizza I mean here and recommend that you try once you arrive in Alexandria is a special pizza that the locals call "eastern pizza". The thing that separate eastern pizza from any other is that it does not have regular pizza dough, the toppings are put on a base of eastern type of pastry that consist of paper-thin layers of delicate dry dough that softens once it is put in the hot oven turning into one layer of rich tender goodness that carries the pizza toppings.

38. DINE AT "FISH MARKET"

When it comes to seafood in Alexandria, everyone has their own favorite restaurant from the long list of Alexandrian seafood restaurants. But to have fresh seafood with a view of the Mediterranean, the place where the food came from, as well as elegance combined together in a fine dining experience is not available in as many restaurants and Fish Market is one of the few places in Alexandria that offer this experience for Alexandrians and tourists alike. Across from the sea, Fish Market is on the second floor which allows its visitors to have a clear unobstructed view of the sea through the windows. With a welcoming atmosphere and an open-air kitchen as well as a counter for the fresh fish placed on ice, a great time is guaranteed for you.

39. GO TO WHITE AND BLUE RESTAURANT

This tip is an alternative for our vegan friends who did not find the previous tip about "Khatab Oasis" very useful. In the White and Blue restaurant, you will find a variety of vegan options that you can enjoy along with the elegant atmosphere of the restaurant. The special décor of the place is very simple and centered on the two colors, as the name suggests, white and blue which gives you a sense of calmness and peace. The restaurant is on the terrace of the Greek Marine Club which gives it the advantage of having a great view in addition to its amazing food that is mostly based on the Greek cuisine.

40. PASS ON THE STANLEY BRIDGE

Stanley Bridge is one of the modern landmarks of Alexandria. If you have ever seen a video or photos of the city, then you must have seen it at least once. Being the first bridge in Alexandria and in all of Egypt to be built over the sea, Stanley Bridge is a source of pride to the city and its people. When you get it Alexandria, it is a must to have at least one picture of yourself on the bridge and have a cup of coffee in one of the many cafes that have the beautiful bridge for a view. Also do not miss a chance to pass by it at night and enjoy the beautiful lights of the bridge as they reflect on the sea water.

41. VISIT THE CATACOMBS OF KOM EL SHOQAFA

The Catacombs of Kom El Shoqafa is an important archaeological historical site of Alexandria's that used to be one of the Seven Wonders of the World in the middle ages. The site consists of a number of Alexandrian tombs and statues along with some objects of the Pharaonic funeral with influences of the Hellenistic and Roman eras. The circular staircase that leads down the catacombs was used to transfer the bodies of the deceased down to their tombs from the 2nd to the 4th centuries AD.

The story of discovering the Catacombs of Kom El Shoqafa in 1900 is quite amusing because the site was discovered by a donkey. The unfortunate animal fell down the access shaft of the catacombs leading to the great discovery of the best site in Alexandria to resemble the nature of the blending of the three civilizations that passed on the city: Pharaonic, Hellenistic, and Roman.

42. RIDE THE TRAM

A few years ago Alexandria took the tram to a whole new level from being an ordinary cheap transportation to being a fully equipped mobile café. The tram café consists of only one very nice cart with carpets, a table for every two chair facing each other and the table, a big screen TV, and WIFI. The tram ticket is not at all expensive considering that you get all that in addition to a ride to your station only for LE 5. Personally, I find great pleasure in riding anything with rails, so if you are like me, you will have so much fun in this café/ transportation experience.

43. VISIT THE UNKNOWN NAVAL SOLDIER MEMORIAL

The Unknown Naval Soldier Memorial is located in Mansheya neighborhood out on the Mediterranean Sea. The memorial is dedicated to every Unknown Soldier who has lost his life in a battle at sea.

Originally, this site was created by the Italian people who lived in Alexandria as honoring to Khedive Ismail, the ruler of Egypt at the time. Many decades after the military coup of 1952 and the revolution that followed, President Mohamed Hosni Mubarak ordered the site to be turned into a memorial for the unknown naval soldier and the statue of the Khedive that used to stand in the site was moved to be a piece of the collection exhibited in the Museum of Fine Arts.

44. RIDE A BIKE IN MAMOURA BEACH

Mamoura Beach is the first thing close to a resort Alexandria had in the 60s of the last century. Esteemed Egyptian Business men and movie starts used to come to this beach to their summer vacations in their villas that lied directly on the sand beach. Nowadays the beach still has its elegance and beauty of the past and it is a great place for families to spend a day by the sea where children and adults can ride a bike on its paved roads and I suggest that you take a chance to enjoy this nice experience between the sandy beach and the beautiful flowers that decorates the sides of the roads. You do not have to have your own bike; you can always rent one from the many bike rental places in Mamoura.

Mamoura beach is located on the eastern side of Alexandria near El Montazah, so it would be a big time saver for you to combine the two visits on the same day.

45. VISIT ST. MINA MONASTERY

St. Mina Monastery is located in the desert western of Alexandria. The monastery of the Coptic Orthodox Church of Alexandria is dedicated to Saint Menas. After the execution of Saint Mina, his sister brought his body to the Church in Alexandria. An angel appeared to Pope Athanasius of Alexandria and ordered him to take the Saiant's body on a camel and head for the western desert. When the Pope followed the order and at a point near water well at the end of lake Mariout, the camel refused to move and that was taken as the sign from God on the place where Saint Mina is to be buried and where the monastery should be built. Saint Mina's body was buried in silver coffin which was then placed into a wooden coffin.

46. VISIT THE SERAPEUM OF ALEXANDRIA

The Serapeum is an ancient Greek temple built in Alexandria while the Ptolemy Kingdom ruled the city and all of Egypt by Ptolemy III Euergtes. The temple was dedicated to Serapis, the god that was invented on the orders of Ptolemy I to unify the Egyptian gods and the Greek gods in this one Graeco-Egyptian god as a policy to guarantee that the Egyptians would not rebel against their Greek rulers as long as they both worship the same god. However, there are also signs in the Serapeum of Harpocrates, the ancient Greek god of silence.

The Serapeum, which is said to have been the largest and most magnificent of all the Greek temples in Alexandria, was built on a rocky hillside which makes it overlooking land and sea alike.

47. GO TO SIDI BISHR MOSQUE

One of the most famous mosques of Alexandria, located in the neighborhood that carries the same name, the Sidi Bishr Mosque overlooks the sea. With a small garden in front of it that the families of the neighborhood use for outings and a yard in front of its doors where children can play, Sidi Bishr Mosque is more than just a place for prayers to be performed in. Personally, growing up as a resident in Sidi Bishr neighborhood, living near the mosque made some of my dearest childhood memories with my father.

If you decide to visit Sidi Bish Mosque and needed a place to catch your breath, check out the one of the many cafés nearby.

48. VISIT SACRED HEART CHURCH

Sacred Heart Church of Alexandria is a Catholic Church that was built in 1924. St. Francis, who served as the patron saint at the Sacred Heart Church and whose name was carried by the many Franciscan schools all around the world, was born in 1181. The church is an attraction for many tourists for its breathtaking religious art, murals, icons, figurines, and amazing stained glass artwork.

The mosaics at the Sacred Heart Church are the combined work of Maurice Josey and Gabriel Pippet. The work on them started in 1921 and it was finished after 12 years of its start.

49. DO NOT FORGET YOUR SUNBLOCK

For the Middle Eastern weather, Alexandria is not considered a city of hot weather at all. However, for Europeans and other people who come from climates that is not used to the sun, it can be rather hot especially if you are planning to come during the summer. The large number of visitors in the summer makes the city over crowded which raises up the heat levels than usual and than it should be in reality.

Even during winter we have some days when it is very sunny, so make sure to have an effective sun block cream with you at all times of your stay in Alexandria.

50. SCHEDULE YOUR TRIP AROUND SPRING

First of all you have to avoid coming during the summer by all means. The city becomes over crowded with holidaymakers in an unimaginable way, you will not be able to enjoy your visit because of that and the awful traffic that results from it. Winter is also not the best choice either because the numerous storms that come to the city every winter; Alexandrians are used to them and the storms are part of their lives, but they can be a bit scary for visitors of the city who are not used to its weather during winter.

The best time to visit Alexandria is either during spring from the end of February to the end of May, or during fall from the end of September to the end of November. In those two times the city riches the peak of its beauty, it is quiet and peaceful, and you will be able to enjoy every minute of your time in Alexandria. We will be waiting for you.

Sohaila Ammar

TOP REASONS TO BOOK THIS TRIP

Beaches: The beaches here are great especially during around the spring time and the beginning of the summer.

Food: The food is very flavorful and divers due to the diversity of the cultures of Alexandria.

Culture: The culture is extremely rich and a unique blend of the many civilizations that passed on Alexandria and ruled it over the centuries.

Monuments: A large number of monuments form at least three ancient civilizations that were built on this ground.

Sohaila Ammar

> TOURIST
GREATER THAN A TOURIST

Visit GreaterThanATourist.com:

http://GreaterThanATourist.com

Sign up for the Greater Than a Tourist Newsletter:

http://eepurl.com/cxspyf

Follow us on Facebook:

https://www.facebook.com/GreaterThanATourist

Follow us on Pinterest:

http://pinterest.com/GreaterThanATourist

Follow us on Instagram:

http://Instagram.com/GreaterThanATourist

Follow on Twitter:

http://twitter.com/ThanaTourist

Sohaila Ammar

> TOURIST
GREATER THAN A TOURIST

Please leave your honest review of this book on Amazon and Goodreads. Thank you. We appreciate your positive and constructive feedback. Thank you.

Sohaila Ammar

NOTES

CPSIA information can be obtained
at www.ICGtesting.com
Printed in the USA
LVHW090852111020
668494LV00007B/2354